SELF-CONFIDENCE FOR MEN

Stop Being the Victim & Boost Your Self-Esteem

John Sonmez

CONTENTS

Self-confidence is a critical factor to success in life. Whether you are looking to climb the corporate ladder, expand your dating options, attract clients or accomplish just about any goal you have, **the degree of self-confidence you possess will often directly contribute to your probability of success.**

(Oh, and yes, you—yes, **even you—can develop a high degree of self-confidence.** You just need to know how. Read on to find out.)

The problem is that while we are taught many things in school, we are not taught self-confidence. In fact, I would say schools and other social environments—even the internet today with the barrage of social media, teaches us how to not have self-confidence rather than how to build it.

But **developing self-confidence is not as difficult as you would think.** It does require a little courage and it definitely requires persistence, but once you understand how self-confidence works and how it can be developed, you'll find that, yes, even you can have self-confidence.

(P.S. If you want to find out what your current self-confidence level is before you read this book, just go to:

https://bulldogmindset.com/confidence-quiz

right now. I highly recommend you take this quiz before you read the rest of this book, so you can get an accurate assessment of where you are beginning.)

WHAT IS CONFIDENCE? WHAT IS SELF-CONFIDENCE?

Before we can talk about how to build self-confidence, we need to understand what confidence and self-confidence are.

We'll begin with the simpler term of confidence.

I've found that **most people don't really understand what confidence is** and what causes confidence. They tend to have the fixed mindset view of confidence as something you either have or don't have. They don't realize the dynamic and contextual nature of confidence itself.

THE SIMPLEST WAY TO THINK OF CONFIDENCE IS TO THINK OF IT AS YOUR ABILITY TO PREDICT OR KNOW AN OUTCOME OR THE POSSIBLE OUTCOMES OF A SITUATION.

Think about how people use the term confidence in a sentence like, "I'm confident that this is the right answer." Or, "I have confidence in the results of the election." Or, "I'm confident you are the best candidate."

Confident means "sure" to a large degree. **If we are confident in something, we are sure of the outcomes or the possible outcomes.**

Now, notice I use the words "possible outcomes" here because all we have to do is know what could or is likely to happen and we can be confident—we don't need to know the exact outcome.

The key here is that we are sure of something. It doesn't matter what it is. We are confident when we are sure.

In fact, the actual definition of *"confident"* is: *"the state of feeling certain about the truth of something."*

Certainty = confidence

CONFIDENCE IS OFTEN CONFUSED WITH ARROGANCE

The two are often confused. I define confidence, or rather self-confidence, as **knowing, or being sure about some aspect of yourself.**

I define arrogance as **trying to convince someone else of something you don't believe about yourself.**

And you can see this in actual observation of people. Two people can say the exact same statements and one person can come off as confident while the other comes off as arrogant. The difference is not what they say, or even how they say it, but **what they believe about the statements they are making.**

A confident person, someone who has true self-confidence, can say "I am the best," and they can say it in such a way that is a matter of fact—an indisputable truth.

An arrogant person can make that same exact statement and say, "I am the best," but you get the impression they are trying to convince you of something they don't truly believe about themselves.

SELF-CONFIDENCE IS BELIEVING OR BEING SURE ABOUT SOMETHING

So, that brings us to self-confidence—what exactly is it?

SELF-CONFIDENCE IS BELIEVING OR BEING SURE ABOUT OURSELVES IN SOME WAY.

But what is a self-confident person sure of?

That's the key; **a self-confident person is sure of their ability to handle a situation and be ok.**

They are confident in themself.

A self-confident person knows whatever situation comes up they can handle it, and that ultimately **they will survive and be ok.** They have been in enough situations to have this sense of self-reliance.

And the important part is: **this is contextual.**

Think about yourself. No matter how much you may feel that you lack confidence, I am sure there is at least one situation in which you feel utmost confidence.

Perhaps you are great at a particular game of some sort. When you play that game, you may not be sure that you will always win, but you are still confident because you know you can adapt to the various situations that come up in the game and play well.

And how did you get there?

Well, you played the game enough times that **you became very aware of the possible outcomes, and of all the outcomes that could occur**, you ultimately realized that you were ok—that you could handle them.

Yes, you might prefer a favorable outcome— we all do—but regardless of what the outcome is, your confidence comes from your certainty in your ability to handle it.

That is what confidence is, and that is how you get it.

A SELF–CONFIDENT PERSON—IN A GIVEN CONTEXT—IS CERTAIN OF THEIR ABILITY TO HANDLE SITUATIONS IN THAT PARTICULAR CONTEXT AND TO BE OK. THAT'S IT.

If you throw that so-called "self-confident person" into a context in which they lack experience or surety, you will find they are likely to lose their confidence. (And you see this happen all the time, by the way.)

WHAT ABOUT PEOPLE WHO ARE TRULY SELF-CONFIDENT?

Now, with that said, some people are truly self-confident.

What I mean by this is that **there are people who are so sure of themselves and their ability to handle any situation**—and be ok— that they can display some degree of confidence in just about any situation life throws at them. These are the people who we could say are confident in the larger context of life itself.

This is the kind of self-confidence you want to develop because it goes deep. This is the kind of self-confidence I'm going to teach you how to develop in the rest of this book.

(Again, don't forget to take the confidence quiz   at
https://bulldogmindset.com/confidence-quiz
to see what your current self-confidence level is.)

DEVELOPING SELF-CONFIDENCE

There are two principal ways we can develop self-confidence.

The first is to **increase our surety** or certainty in our abilities to handle a particular set of possible situations.

The second is to **increase our feeling of being OK**, regardless of the outcome of a situation.

Again, we can apply this contextually, but we can also apply this to life to become a more self-confident individual, regardless of the situation.

Let's start with how we can apply this in a context so that we can gain confidence in certain abilities or aspects of our lives, and then we can take a look at the bigger picture and see how to expand that to all areas of life.

RUNNING A RACE

Before I talk about exactly how to build confidence in a context or situation, I want to tell you a story about my first time running a half-marathon.

When I signed up for my first half-marathon, I had already been running for a few years and had been progressively been tackling some longer and longer distances.

My longest runs were around 10 miles, so I figured I could probably make it for a 13.1-mile run—probably.

So, on a whim, I decided to sign up for the San Diego Rock-and-Roll Half-Marathon—**the day before the race.**

Now, I had done some 5k races before, but I had never run a half-marathon, and I had never signed up for a race this big. You can probably guess that my confidence was pretty low.

I wasn't sure what to do. I wasn't sure where I needed to be and what time. I wasn't sure if I was going to end up in the right place. **I wasn't even sure if I could finish the race,** or if I did, if I would get a good time.

Just about everything about the situation of running a half-marathon was new to me and it made me nervous.

Really, the only thing I had going for me was that I had run some longer distances and had been training pretty hard. I also knew from the past that I had often gotten myself in over my head in many situations, but somehow always came through and learned from them. This would be a learning experience.

Long story short, I showed up and ran the San Diego Rock-and-Roll Half-Marathon and finished in a decent time of just over 2 hours, but… I hadn't been confident at all.

Now, fast forward to today, and I've run a bunch of half-marathons and even a full marathon.

I'm used to running these kinds of races. I know what to expect. I know how the race will generally go. I know what kind of hurdles and obstacles I am likely to face along the way. And, I've had outstanding performances in the past. **I am sure of my ability to run a race and to handle any situation that is likely to occur during the race.**

My confidence in running long-distance endurance events is very high.

It's high because I've been there, seen that, done that, gotten the t-shirt (literally), and know that whatever happens, I'll be ok.

How did I gain that confidence?

Again, in primarily two ways: **experience and positive outcomes.**

DEVELOPING SELF-CONFIDENCE THROUGH EXPERIENCE

THE EASIEST AND BEST WAY TO DEVELOP SELF-CONFIDENCE IS THROUGH EXPERIENCE.

The main reason I became confident in running half-marathons and marathons was that I accumulated a bunch of experience running those kinds of races.

I got to the point where **I knew what was likely to happen** during a race, from start till finish, and **I knew I could handle and overcome any of the obstacles in my way.** The experience got me to the point where I wasn't sure of the outcome, but I was sure of my ability to handle every step along the way and to deal with any potential outcome which was likely to occur.

So, one surefire way to develop confidence is through experience.

As Arnold says, *"There are no shortcuts— everything is reps, reps, reps."*

IF YOU WANT TO GAIN CONFIDENCE, YOU CAN GAIN IT BY DOING WHATEVER YOU WANT TO GAIN CONFIDENCE IN, OVER AND OVER AGAIN.

One of the most common confidence questions I get is from men asking me how to have confidence with women. **One of the most attractive traits that a man can have is to be confident**, so naturally, guys want to appear confident to women and be confident around women.

As a young man, I struggled in this area as well. I was afraid to talk to women. I was afraid to approach them. I lacked confidence in this area and it showed.

So, what did I do to overcome this fear and gain the confidence to approach and converse with women and display confidence in their presence?

Well, if you are following along so far, I'm sure you can guess... yes, that's right, **I gained experience by approaching and talking to lots of women until I was no longer afraid** and instead was confident. (And yes, it took a long time and involved a very large number of reps.)

You can fake a lot of things in life, but remember guys, **the one thing you can't fake is confidence.** Confidence is something you either have or you don't have.

Again, one guaranteed way to build confidence is through gaining experience by subjecting yourself to the thing or activity you want to gain confidence in, over and over again.

HOW TO GAIN CONFIDENCE THROUGH EXPERIENCE

You might be thinking, "Yes, John, I get it– you can gain confidence through experience, but that's easier said than done. How do you actually gain experience and how do you deal with things like fear and anxiety that get in the way?"

Let's start with the basics.

First, you need to **understand and believe that this process will automatically work if you apply it and that you don't need to focus on or worry about results**, because results will come.

You essentially have to do what I call **trusting the process.**

This means **divorcing the outcome from the process that gets you to the outcome.**

This is essential because if you are constantly worrying about the outcome, you are going to have a difficult time just doing what you need to do in order to gain experience, and you'll likely feel like it's not working.

Instead, what I want you to do is **forget about results**—for now—and instead just **focus on getting as much experience as possible.**

One of my good friends, Dan Martell, posted a video on Facebook recently showing a kid attempting to do a back-flip 260 times.

After 260 tries, he finally nails the back-flip with no padding or other support. You can watch his progress over the tries as he gets better and better.

THE POINT HERE ISN'T THAT IT'S IMPRESSIVE THAT HE TRIED SO MANY TIMES, BUT RATHER THAT, YOU AND I ARE LIKELY ONLY 260 TRIES AWAY FROM BEING ABLE TO DO A BACK-FLIP. HOW CRAZY IS THAT?

What other things in life are you only X number of tries away from?

Let me put it this way: you are ONLY X number of experiences away from being confident at Y.

If you are willing to put in the tries, you WILL get the result. Let me repeat that.

IF you are WILLING to put in the tries, you WILL get the RESULT.

So, the question is: are you willing to put in the tries?

If so, the process is fairly simple. Let's break it down right here.

THE PROCESS OF GAINING CONFIDENCE THROUGH EXPERIENCE

Step 1: Pick the goal

First, pick the thing you want to gain confidence in—easy enough.

Step 2: Determine the action

Next, figure out ways to gain experience in that thing. Again, seems obvious, but so many people skip this step.

Let's take a look at a few examples, so you can see how it's done.

If you want to gain confidence in your ability to speak on stage, you can do so by speaking on stage.

If you want to gain confidence in your ability to draw, you can do so by drawing.

If you want to gain confidence in talking to women, you can do so by talking to women.

Yes, I know it's obvious, but most things in life are pretty obvious. Most people know how to solve all the problems they have in life, but they never take the time to sit and think about it.

Step 3: Define the process

Now you need to actually commit to a number of repetitions you are going to do BEFORE you evaluate your progress.

So, figure out whatever it was that you needed to do to gain experience in Step 2 and COMMIT to doing that action X number of times.

How do you figure out what X is? Simple.

You ask yourself this one important question: **How many times would I, or someone else—sometimes it helps to think in terms of someone else—need to do X action to guarantee success?** (And in this case, success means gaining confidence.)

For example, when I was starting my YouTube channel, I had a goal of gaining 100,000 subscribers. I thought to myself,

"How many videos would I need to make to guarantee I'd have 100,000 subscribers?"

I ended up coming up with the idea that if I produced 2,000 videos, it would be difficult for me to not have at least 100,000 subscribers.

Was this an absolutely accurate guess? No, I kind of just winged it based on looking at other channels that had 100,000 or more subscribers and what I thought based on my experience.

Do the same here.

Maybe you feel like getting on stage 100 times would give you confidence in your ability to speak on stage. Maybe it's 20, or 1,000, it doesn't really matter, except that it needs to be a goal you can achieve and commit to.

Step 4: Do the work

Now is the part where you put your head down and do, do, do. Don't worry about results, just do.

Whatever you committed to in Step 3, you are going to do until you've fulfilled that commitment.

Step 5: Evaluate and adjust

Now that you've accomplished the goal, it's time to bring your head above water to see where you are at.

Honestly, evaluate yourself and ask whether you've gained the confidence you were seeking. If you did, great, if you didn't ask the following question:

Did I fail because I needed more reps or because I was doing the wrong thing?

It's critical to know whether you were on the right road, but just didn't take it far enough, or if you were on the wrong road altogether.

If you made progress, you were probably on the right road and should take it further, but you should also look and see if there is a way you can gain the experience more effectively at a faster rate.

If you didn't make any real progress, you are probably doing the wrong thing.

All of this might seem stupidly simple, but if it's so simple, why haven't you done it already?

WHAT ABOUT FEAR AND ANXIETY?

One of the biggest objections I get to the process of using repetitions to gain experience and, as a result, confidence, is that fear or anxiety holds you back from actually doing the action in the first place.

It can seem like a catch-22 where the lack of confidence is what stops you from taking the action, but not taking the action is what prevents you from ever gaining confidence.

So, how do you break this cycle?

Courage.

Yes, courage is the answer.

I used to be a very fearful person. I used to let my fears get the best of me.

I was afraid to talk to people—especially girls.

I was afraid to ride on airplanes, rollercoasters, and anything that could kill me.

I was afraid to move out of my comfort zone.

I thought that fear would eventually dissipate if I just gave it a time or if I just somehow got confidence, but guess what?

It never happened. Instead, the **fear got worse and worse and took over more and more of my life—that's what fear does.**

So, what is the solution?

Again, courage.

COURAGE IS NOT THE LACK OF FEAR, BUT AS NELSON MANDELA ONCE SAID, IT IS AN ACTION DESPITE FEAR.

We can't be courageous unless we are also afraid. So, to be brave is to be afraid, but to take action anyway.

I wish I could give you some magic pill that would make it so you wouldn't have to confront and face your fears to gain experience, or some kind of magic salve that cured you of fear altogether, but I can't. **Only YOU can face your fears and you must do it alone.**

So, the answer to dealing with fear and anxiety with regard to gaining the experience you need to build confidence is to just plow ahead and do what needs to be done.

Now, one thing that can help you do this is to have the **right expectations** and to have **freedom from the outcome.**

First, your expectations should be that it will suck, it will be uncomfortable, and perhaps even embarrassing, but that it's ok. That is the price you have to pay for the eventual result you want. When you think this way, you will be much more likely to face and confront your fear, because you will stop bargaining and start realizing that it is simply a price you must pay if you want the result you are after.

When you expect things will suck, you are more likely to do them and less likely to give up, rather than when you expect things to be easy and fun and find out they are not.

Freedom from the outcome is a concept we've already alluded to. It is the same as divorcing the results from the process that gets them, or trusting the process.

WHEN YOU ARE FACING FEARS, IT'S BEST TO NOT WORRY ABOUT THE RESULT, BUT TO COUNT JUST TAKING ACTION AS A "WIN" FOR YOU.

With guys I've coached on overcoming their fears and anxiety about women, I've often told them that as soon as they say "hi" (or anything), they've already succeeded and won, because they showed and demonstrated courage.

Give yourself a big win if you talk to the girl, step on the stage, enter the race, take the leap, make the pitch, play the game, make the attempt, fill in the blank.

This is also a powerful technique that I call a **context shift.** You are shifting the context from you trying to accomplish some task or have confidence, to simply taking some action for the purpose of moving forward.

When I coach new YouTubers on creating videos, I tell them the goal is not to make a good video, it's only to get on camera and put yourself out into the world. Every time you do this, you are gaining experience and moving forward. That's all we are focusing on right now.

I'll wrap this section up by saying one last thing on the topic.

If fear is the only thing standing between you and your goals in life, someday you are going to have to face those fears if you are going to ever achieve your goals, so you might as well get it over with and face them NOW.

GAINING CONFIDENCE THROUGH POSITIVE OUTCOMES

Remember way back when I said there are two primary ways to gain confidence?

(There's actually a third, but we'll get to that later.)

I said the experience was one—and we've already beat that dead horse—but now let's talk about another, perhaps even faster way, positive outcome.

NOTHING CAN BOOST YOUR CONFIDENCE MORE THAN HAVING GOOD RESULTS IN THE THINGS YOU ARE TRYING TO DO.

The thing to understand here is that it's all relative, and you can create your own positive outcomes by changing the goal, or context, as we did in the fear example earlier.

Positive outcomes greatly boost our confidence, because once we've already succeeded, we usually feel like we can succeed again. (Although sometimes our self-doubt is so strong that we attribute all our successes to luck—which can also be a problem.)

So, one great way to build confidence is to **get positive outcomes in the pursuit of the things we are trying to gain confidence in.**

Many times, people who seem naturally confident seem that way not because they are naturally confident, but because the first few attempts they made at a thing were met with great success, and it created this virtuous cycle where their boosted confidence led to an inhibition of fear and thus more success.

The most common example of this you see is in guys that have success with women.

Many times, these naturally successful guys will have some trait, perhaps good looks, popularity or athleticism, which made their initial encounters with women successful. This led to them becoming more confident with women, which led to them having more success and thus more confidence and more experience, and the cycle continued.

You can benefit from this same process by setting yourself up for positive outcomes.

ENGINEERING POSITIVE OUTCOMES

I mentioned earlier that positive outcomes were relative, and it's true. Let me give you an example.

Bear with me, I'm going to talk about distance running again...

So, I'm about 220 lbs, 6'3" and **not exactly built at all like a distance runner.** I look a lot more like a linebacker than a distance runner. I don't have any dreams of ever setting any kind of world record, competing in the Olympics or even ever winning a half-marathon, marathon or other distance events. (Although I recently did win a 5k for my age group. Woot!)

Anyway, if I set a goal of running what many people would consider to be a very fast and competitive time in a half-marathon, I would come up each time sorely disappointed, because I wouldn't even be close. I would have an extremely negative outcome.

But, fortunately for me, **I don't set a goal of competing with distance runners** who tip the scale at 130 lbs and have been running distance since they were in elementary school. Instead, **I set reasonable goals that are meaningful to me.**

For example, one of my first half-marathon goals was to get a time under 2 hours. This was something I felt was a good goal for a beginning runner—especially for one weighing 220 lbs.

That's me running the LA Rock-and-Roll Halloween Half-Marathon

I achieved that goal and then I set a goal of getting under 1:55. Which I also achieved.

Currently, I'm striving to hit a full marathon goal time of under 4 hours—which, hopefully in a week, I'll achieve as well.

The key is that **I am purposely setting myself up for positive outcomes by picking goals that are achievable and yet still meaningful to me.**

Running a better race and having a faster personal best time is progress and I consider it a positive outcome.

But, again, it's all relative. Someone else might think my times are slow and suck. I could compare my times and goals to those of the top distance runners in the world, and I could see my results as failures and negative outcomes.

But, if I did that, I would not gain any confidence in my running and it's doubtful I'd continue to run.

SO, IF YOU WANT TO GAIN CONFIDENCE, FIGURE OUT WAYS TO ENGINEER POSITIVE OUTCOMES FOR YOURSELF.

Figure out achievable goals you can set for yourself and push yourself to achieve those goals. Don't judge your results on the eventual results you'd like to get. Give yourself a big win just for taking action, just for getting out there and doing what you are supposed to do.

If you know that continued action (reps, reps, and more reps) is going to get you to your larger goal eventually, consider each time you take action a win, and treat it as such. Doing so will let you put a few notches in your belt and will bolster your confidence.

(Want to know what your current confidence rating is from 1 to 100? Take the confidence quiz at https://bulldogmindset.com/confidence-quiz to find out.)

CAUTION: THE DANGER OF POSITIVE OUTCOMES

Now, I feel like I should warn you there is a danger of positive outcomes that comes a little too easily and that is: overconfidence.

While positive outcomes are good and can pump up our confidence level, **sometimes if those positive outcomes come too easily and we "get lucky" in achieving them, we can achieve the desired outcome of increasing our confidence, but that confidence can indeed be false confidence.**

You see this all the time in what we sometimes refer to as beginner's luck. A person tries a thing that they have little experience or skill at. They are met with sudden undeserved success and they get an inflated perception of their own abilities.

THE DANGER IN THIS IS THAT OVERCONFIDENCE AND FALSE CONFIDENCE CAN BE GREAT INHIBITORS TO LONG-TERM CONFIDENCE AND THE OVERALL FEELING OF SELF-CONFIDENCE, BECAUSE AS THEY SAY, "PRIDE GOETH BEFORE A FALL."

When our confidence is not based on experience but is solely based on positive outcomes, a sudden negative outcome can evaporate all that confidence immediately—like getting punched in the stomach and getting the wind knocked out of you.

The antidote for this problem is to **make sure your confidence at its core is based on actual skill and experience,** and that you honestly evaluate your successes and positive outcomes to understand why they occurred. Did they happen because you were skilled, or because you were just lucky, or perhaps some combination of both?

Two books come to mind that address this issue. One of them is, *Thinking In Bets*, by the former professional poker player Annie Duke, and the other is, *What I Learned Losing a Million Dollars*.

In *Thinking In Bets*, Annie helps you to understand the role of luck and skill in all outcomes in life and gives you some tools to evaluate the makeup of the two.

What I Learned Losing a Million Dollars shares a firsthand story of overconfidence, how it can come about and the destructive effects it can have if unchecked.

A THIRD METHOD OF GAINING CONFIDENCE

Most of the time a combination of experience and engineered positive outcomes are going to be the two most effective ways to gain confidence, but **there is a third tool** that can aid both the acquisition of experience and the achievement of positive outcomes: **practice and preparation.**

Sometimes, we can't even gain direct experience in what we are trying to gain confidence in because we just don't have the opportunity, or the price of failure is too costly.

Consider the futility of becoming confident and gaining skill in military combat by being in military combat situations.

First, the opportunities to "go to war" are pretty limited, and second, well, the costs of not being good or confident are very, very high.

In just about all situations—but especially these kinds—**practice and preparation can bolster confidence by simulating the experience and priming us to expect and achieve a positive outcome when we do get the chance to gain experience.**

I don't have to run a marathon to gain confidence in my ability to run one on race day. Instead, I can practice and train hard. I can simulate race day by going over the course and doing a walk-through of the sequence of events that will occur and where I'll need to go and be at certain times. I can do a rehearsal of a marathon race to build my confidence ahead of time for when I am in the actual experience.

Now, this doesn't mean you can completely substitute practice and preparation for real experience and real positive outcomes, but you can achieve a top level of confidence simply by being prepared for the real experience or event—especially if your simulations are good.

This was me in the past before I even
considered "self-confidence" as an option.

APPLYING PRACTICE AND PREPARATION TO BUILD CONFIDENCE

To use this tool properly, you need to **plan adequately and prepare for how to best practice** whatever it is you want to gain confidence in.

One of the most effective things you can do to increase your skill level and build competence, which will translate into confidence, is called **deliberate practice.**

There are two excellent books on deliberate practice which I highly recommend.

Mastery by Robert Greene
and *Peak* by Anders Ericsson and Robert Pool. Both books talk about deliberate practice, and how focusing on the right kind of practice can lead to phenomenal results and mastery of a particular set of skills.

ONE INTERESTING ANALYSIS
FROM THESE BOOKS IS A
STUDY DONE ON CHESS
PLAYERS WHICH SHOWED
THAT THOSE CHESS PLAYERS
WHO FOCUSED ON DELIBERATE
PRACTICE, FOR EXAMPLE
WATCHING CHESS END GAMES
AND PRACTICING THEM,
INSTEAD OF FOCUSING ON
PRACTICE BY ACTUALLY
PLAYING MORE CHESS,
IMPROVED MUCH FASTER
THAN THOSE WHOSE
STRATEGY FOR IMPROVEMENT
WAS PLAYING MORE CHESS.

A similar study was done with musicians who played scales and technical pieces versus those who played songs they knew over and over again.

The important takeaway here is that you need to specifically practice a part of the skill that you'd like to improve over and over again to gain mastery, which will greatly increase your confidence.

So, focus on figuring out specific component pieces of whatever you are trying to master, and practice them over and over again to gain the competency.

A good example would be the Muay Thai training I am doing.

Yes, sparring and fighting gain experience and thus confidence for me, but if I spar and fight without practicing my specific punches, kicks and combinations first, I won't maximize the benefits because I'll pretty much get my ass whooped, which will not increase my confidence very much.

But, if I focus on doing specific training and deliberate practice in class, I can develop the confidence that I know how to throw a good Muay Thai kick, block and attack, or throw a combination. That will lead to me feeling more confident overall in a sparring match or real fight, and will lead to more positive outcomes which will further increase my confidence.

GETTING BACK TO SELF-CONFIDENCE

Ok, now that we understand how to develop contextual confidence or situational confidence, we can take these same principles and ideas and apply them at a larger scale to develop an overall, all-encompassing self-confidence which is less contextual in nature.

Now it's time to become a bulldog bad-ass.

Remember the two components of self-confidence?

First, we have to be **certain of our ability to handle a situation** that presents itself, and second, we need **to feel like regardless of the outcome, we'll be OK.**

We can gain this kind of confidence through experience and positive outcomes—magnified by preparation and practice.

We just have to apply all of this to the larger context of life.

Let's break it down step-by-step so we can see how we can utilize everything we've learned so far.

GAINING LIFE EXPERIENCE

WE CAN BECOME SURE OF OUR ABILITY TO HANDLE ANY SITUATION WE FACE SIMPLY BY FACING MANY SITUATIONS.

I know it seems pretty obvious, but again I have to ask you if it's so obvious why aren't you doing this already?

The issue is that it is much more easily said than done. It's tough to face many situations in life because it involves facing our fears and going out of our comfort zones—a lot.

Let me give you another example from my own life.

One thing that truly increased my overall self-confidence was traveling to many foreign countries—especially ones where English wasn't the spoken language and I had to figure out how to get around.

The first time I left the United States to go somewhere foreign, **I had no idea what to expect.** I had no idea what I would face, what international travel would be like, what the people would be like, or even how I was going to communicate and get to my ultimate destination.

It was a pretty scary experience, but **I forced myself to go through it,** and when I did, I became more certain of myself in the respect that I could handle dealing with this kind of trip into an unknown land and that whatever happened, I'd figure out a solution and ultimately be OK.

After that first experience, I traveled again and again to different countries over the years and as a result, **I've increased my overall self-confidence as a person** because I know that **I've dealt with many sticky, scary and stressful situations and have somehow prevailed and survived.**

I have confidence in my ability to adapt, figure out solutions, and make things work out.

Likewise, I've done a lot of other things in my life that scared me at first but have ultimately led to a feeling of being able to handle anything that life can throw at me.

Here's a shortlist of examples:

- Quitting my job to run my own business
- Putting myself on video and putting it out into the world
- Writing books and putting them out into the world
- Creating and selling online courses and asking people for money
- Talking to and striking up conversations with total strangers
- Talking to women and teaching guys how to do the same
- Running a marathon
- Joining a Muay Thai class
- Lifting weights and transforming my body
- Facing my fears and going on crazy theme park rides
- Investing in real estate by buying properties
- Getting on stage and talking at conferences and events
- Doing acting and modeling
- Traveling around the world
- Much more

The more of these kinds of life experiences you bring into your life, the more self-confident you will become because you will develop surety in yourself to handle just about any situation you encounter.

THE ROLE OF EXTERNAL VALIDATION

Another important part of bolstering this self-confidence is **getting rid of the dependence on others for validation**—moving from external validation to internal or self-validation.

When you rely on external validation, you can't be sure of yourself because your feelings and senses of wellbeing are not in your control, but are in the control of others.

Many people who suffer from some self-confidence issues or very low self-confidence do so primarily because **they are overly concerned about what other people think about them.** They are trying to get approval from other people so that they can feel good about themselves as a person. Their conception of other people's opinion of them is more important than their own opinion of themselves.

IF YOU ARE DEPENDENT ON WHAT OTHER PEOPLE THINK OF YOU AND WORRIED ABOUT THEIR APPROVAL, HOW CAN YOU POSSIBLY BE SURE OF YOURSELF? HOW CAN YOU POSSIBLY HAVE SELF-CONFIDENCE?

We can all fall into this trap—in fact, society teaches us to value the opinion of others more than our own opinions.

We can break free from this prison by developing a stoic mindset—what I would call <u>the Bulldog Mindset.</u>

We can do this by **learning the skills of self-reliance and by seeking out and accomplishing goals** we set for ourselves in life. As we set out to achieve our goals in life and we realize we can achieve them, we become much more self-reliant and care less about what other people think of us.

When we begin to trust ourselves and our own opinions and values, we reject the need to seek approval from an outside source.

Knowing what we do and who we are makes us happy. That is enough for us, and so we become internally motivated, much more certain of ourselves and, as a result, much more self-confident.

This, of course, is all easier said than done, but that's where **a focus on personal development can really help to move you forward** in this direction.

Read books like Tony Robbins's classic *Awaken the Giant Within* to help you gain a healthy belief in yourself and to understand the basic human needs which we all need to be fulfilled.

REALIZING YOU ARE GOING TO BE OK

Another way we can apply the contextual principles we've already talked about for building genuine self-confidence is by **engineering both positive and negative outcomes** to build the overarching belief that **no matter what happens, we are going to be OK.**

It might seem a little weird that I'm talking about generating negative outcomes, but in order to build unshakable self-confidence we need to understand that good or bad, positive or negative, ultimately we'll be OK.

Think of it this way. Suppose you are in the situation of talking to a stranger for the first time—perhaps the very thought of it makes you nervous.

If you have the mindset that no matter what happens, even if you are rejected, you are going to be OK and you'll be able to handle the situation, don't you think you'll be much more confident taking the risk?

The problem is, most of the time we are worried about the results. We are worried that we'll get rejected, or that we'll lose or fail or something will go wrong and then we think "what then?"

But if we've faced fear and rejection, if we've had negative and positive outcomes from things we've done in life, and regardless of the outcome, we've somehow come out OK, then we are much more likely to be self-confident in any situation, even new or uncomfortable ones.

This is where **it is important to create goals in your life and achieve them.** You want to engineer some positive outcomes so that you can feel confident that when you put your mind to something, you can do it, and you can do it on your own, regardless of what other people think.

I gained a huge amount of self-confidence when I beat the odds, did what other people thought was impossible, and became a successful entrepreneur, running my own businesses.

But, on the other side of the equation, you should also **put yourself in situations where you will have some kind of negative outcome.**

Go ahead and put yourself into the public eye, where you will surely get your share of hate.

When I first started writing blog posts or making YouTube videos, **I got plenty of nasty emails**, comments and messages, and I still do. It was a wake-up call that not everyone is nice and accepting. Some people are just assholes, and the world might not be as friendly of a place as I would have liked.

But... guess what?

All of that hatred spewed at me, did it actually physically hurt me in any way? Was I emotionally traumatized for life? Did it even matter at all—unless I let it?

No to all of those things.

I could take the worst the internet had to offer me, and I was still OK. (I was more than OK because I was actually taking action and making more of myself while other people were sitting on their asses judging me!)

The same goes for facing rejection. There is an influential book called *Rejection Proof*, where the author details his story of going out and trying to get rejected by people. It's a great story, but the lessons are invaluable.

If you are willing to face rejection, you will become immunized against rejection. You will realize it's not really that bad, and as a result, you'll start to feel like whatever happens, you'll be OK, which will of course increase your self-confidence.

WHAT ABOUT PRACTICE AND PREPARATION?

Can we use those tools to not only contextually increase our confidence, but to do so to increase our overall self-confidence?

Absolutely.

This looks like increasing our overall skills and character—basically **personal development.**

If you become physically stronger and more physically fit, you are going to feel more confident and more prepared to take on the physical challenges of life.

Believe me when I say that **knowing that I have sub 10% body fat and can run 26.2 miles makes me pretty self-confident**— sometimes a little cocky!

If you become mentally tough, develop the Bulldog Mindset and can withstand pain, if you have discipline and fortitude, you'll be pretty confident that you can handle and deal with whatever trials and tests life throws your way.

If you have learned to **master your emotions**, and you have learned interpersonal and people skills, and you can communicate well, you'll again feel equipped to handle situations in life when you have to deal with, negotiate with, or influence others.

If you know how to **handle and manage money,** and you've had success with your personal finances, you'll feel confident that you can deal with any financial difficulties that will come up in life.

I could go on and on, but I think you get the point.

ULTIMATELY, THE MORE YOU DEVELOP YOURSELF, YOUR CHARACTER AND YOUR SKILLS, THE MORE YOU'LL FIND THAT YOU'LL BE ABLE TO BELIEVE IN YOUR CAPABILITIES, WHICH WILL TRANSLATE DIRECTLY INTO A HIGH LEVEL OF GENERAL SELF-CONFIDENCE.

WATCH OUT FOR THE BULLSHIT

I would be doing you a major disservice if I didn't warn you about the bullshit that is out there with regards to self-confidence.

If you search the internet, or you look for books on self-confidence, many "experts" will tell you things like:

- Dress nicely
- Groom yourself
- Think positive thoughts about yourself
- Use affirmations
- Stop thinking negatively
- Stand up straight
- Smile
- Etc.

Don't get me wrong. These are all good things—and you should do them—but, **true confidence can't be faked or manipulated.**

YOU CAN NEVER SIMPLY "ACT" CONFIDENT—IT JUST DOESN'T WORK.

Trust me, from coaching plenty of guys who want to "appear" more confident, I can tell you it is not possible. Instead, focus on actually becoming more self-confident, which you now know how to do.

Many things in life can be faked. I love the phrase "fake it until you make it." I've applied fake it until you make it many times in my life, but confidence cannot and will not be faked.

So, buck up for the long haul, practice building some situational confidence at first, then take the concepts you've learned here and apply them to your life.

I'm going to leave you with **10 final tips** to help you build your self-confidence based on everything we've talked about here.

10 TIPS TO BUILD SELF-CONFIDENCE

1. Do one thing that scares you every single day.
2. Make a daily habit of reading personal development books.
3. Get into a daily habit of physical exercise that challenges you.
4. Develop at least one skill in which you have high degrees of situational confidence.
5. Talk to strangers as often as you can.
6. Write, blog, make YouTube videos, start a podcast or do something else to put yourself into the public eye and face criticism.
7. Pick clear goals out for your life and make daily progress towards achieving them.
8. When confronted with two paths in life, purposely take the hard road.
9. Visualize the person you want to become every day. Act like you are already that person.
10. Stop caring what other people think, care about what YOU think instead.

To see what your confidence level is right now and to get even more tips on how to improve it, go to https://bulldogmindset.com/confidence-quiz.

Made in the USA
Columbia, SC
01 June 2025

58748092R00039